AF413179

Advanced Color by Math for 5th Graders

Children's Math Books

Speedy Publishing LLC

40 E. Main St. #1156

Newark, DE 19711

www.speedypublishing.com

Copyright 2018

Let's master math and creativity with these excersises.

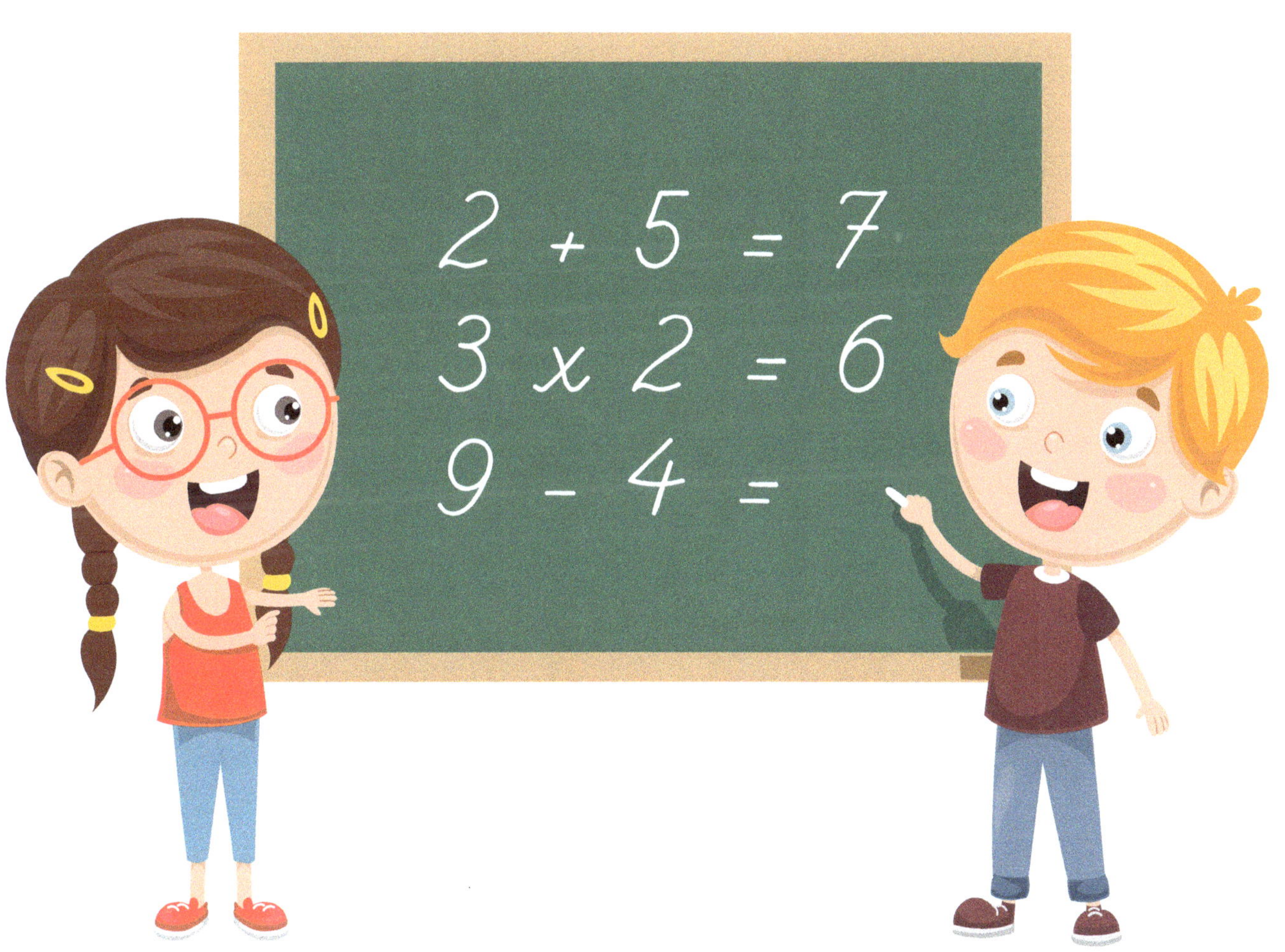

Multiplication

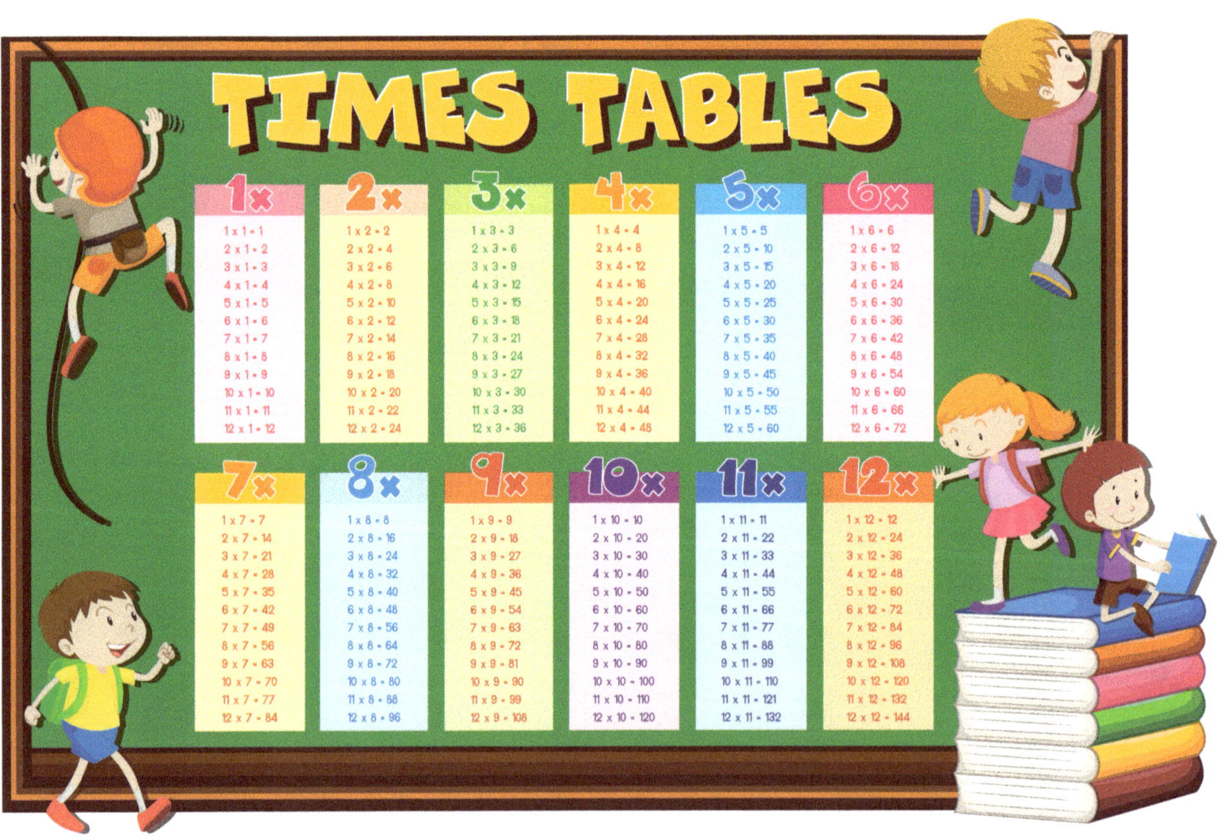

COLOR BY MATH

Complete each math problem and color the page!

COLOR BY MATH

Complete each math problem and color the page!

COLOR BY MATH

Cat

Complete each math problem and color the page!

COLOR BY MATH

Balloon

Complete each math problem and color the page!

MDAS
(Multiplication, Division, Addition And Subtraction)

COLOR BY MATH

Circus

Complete each math problem and color the page!

Duck

Complete each math problem and color the page!

algebra

COLOR BY MATH

Ladybug

Complete each math problem and color the page!

COLOR BY MATH

Air Balloon

Complete each math problem and color the page!

COLOR BY MATH

Complete each math problem and color the page!

COLOR BY MATH

Complete each math problem and color the page!

COLOR BY MATH

Forest

Complete each math problem and color the page!

COLOR BY MATH

Star

Complete each math problem and color the page!

$$3.2 \times 2$$

$$2.1 \times 4$$

$$y + 33 = 52 \times 3$$

$$3.2 \times 3$$

$$8.5 \times 5$$

$$21y = 30 + 33$$

$$y + 34 = 31 \times 4$$

$$1.1 \times 5$$

$$5.4 \times 2$$

COLOR BY MATH

Complete each math problem and color the page!

Done with solving,
time to relax!

Color the pages!
Enjoy!

Let's get started!

COLOR BY NUMBER

Use the codes below to color the picture.

1 - light blue   2 - blue   3 - green   4 - dark green
5 - yellow   6 - gray   7 - black   8 - brown

COLOR BY NUMBER

Use the codes below to color the picture.

1 - light blue   2 - blue   3 - green   4 - dark green
5 - yellow   6 - orange   7 - red   8 - brown

COLOR BY NUMBER

Use the codes below to color the picture.

1 - light blue   2 - gray   3 - green   4 - dark green   5 - yellow
6 - orange   7 - red   8 - brown   9 - pink   10 - black

COLOR BY NUMBER

Use the codes below to color the picture.

1 - white   2 - light blue   3 - gray   4 - green
5 - yellow   6 - orange   7 - brown   8 - dark green

COLOR BY NUMBER

Use the codes below to color the picture.

1 - light blue 2 - orange 3 - brown 4 - green 5 - dark green
6 - yellow 7 - beige 8 - dark blue 9 - pink 10 - gray

COLOR BY NUMBER

Use the codes below to color the picture.

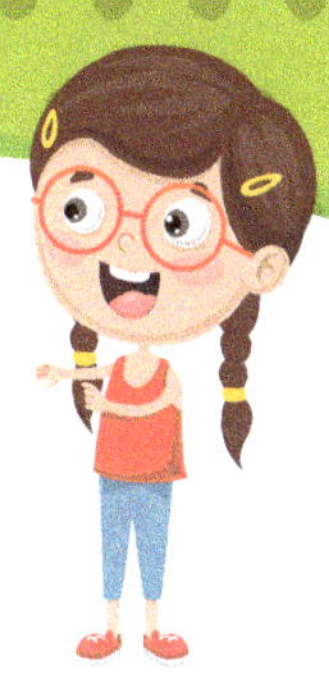

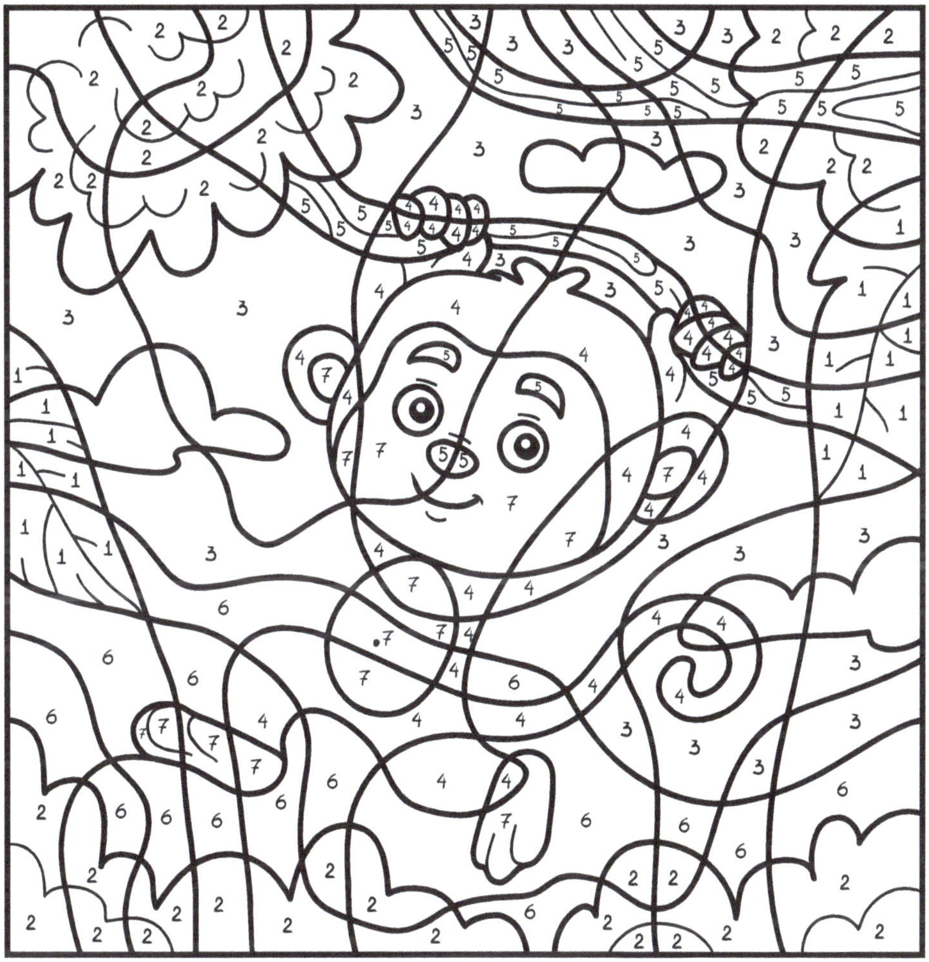

1 - green 2 - dark green 3 - light blue 4 - orange
5 - brown 6 - blue 7 - beige

COLORING PAGES

Color the mandala animals.

COLORING PAGES

Color the mandala animals.

COLORING PAGES

Color the mandala animals.

COLORING PAGES

Color the mandala animals.

COLORING PAGES

Color the mandala animals.

COLORING PAGES

Color the mandala animals.

COLORING PAGES

Color the mandala animals.

COLORING PAGES

Color the mandala animals.

COLORING PAGES

Color the mandala animals.

www.ingramcontent.com/pod-product-compliance
Lightning Source LLC
Chambersburg PA
CBHW040737150726